HORNS, ANTLERS, FANGS, AND TUSKS

BY MARK J. RAUZON

For Kendra Marcus

Acknowledgements

Special thanks to the following people for the use of their photographs: Craig S. Harrison for the black rhinoceros on page 8 and the fighting warthogs on page 21, Larry Lipsky/Tom Stack & Associates for the dueling key deer on page 14, Kevin Schafer & Martha Hill/Tom Stack & Associates for the African elephant on page 22, and Karl W. Kenyon for the walrus on page 23.

Library of Congress Cataloging in Publication Data   Rauzon, Mark J.   Horns, antlers, fangs, and tusks / Mark J. Rauzon.   p.   cm.
Summary: Describes the appearance and uses of different types of animal headgear.   ISBN 0-688-10230-1   ISBN 0-688-10231-X (lib. bdg.)
1. Animal weapons—Juvenile literature.   2. Horns—Juvenile literature.   3. Teeth—Juvenile literature.   4. Tusks—Juvenile literature.
[1. Animal weapons.   2. Horns.   3. Teeth.   4. Tusks.]   I. Title.   QL940.R38 1991   599.057—dc20   90-49726   CIP   AC

LOTHROP, LEE & SHEPARD BOOKS   NEW YORK

HIPPOPOTAMUSES ▲ **▼ AXIS DEER**

BLACK BUCK

OCELOT

THERE ARE MANY KINDS OF ANIMALS IN THE WORLD. No matter how different they look or act, some things about them are the same. All animals need to get food and all animals need to protect themselves.

Horns, antlers, fangs, and tusks may look different, but animals use them to do the same things: to eat and to fight.

JACOB'S
SHEEP

GREATER KUDU

HORNS

Only animals with hooves—cattle, goats, sheep, and antelope—can grow horns. Some horns are curly and others are straight. Some are short and others are long. All of them have only one point.

Horns grow in pairs from bony knobs on an animal's skull. They are made of keratin, the same material that hooves and toenails are made of.

DALL SHEEP: EWE AND LAMB

Female hoofed animals may have small horns or none at all. Males have big horns. They use them to protect themselves and their families from other animals and to fight each other when it's time to mate.

DALL SHEEP: RAM

Horns grow a little every year. The older an animal is, the bigger its horns are. The size of this ram's horns tell us he is middle-aged, about 10 years old.

Sometimes "horns" can fool you. The ones on a rhinoceros's nose are not true horns at all. They are masses of super-strong hair packed together.

BLACK RHINOCEROS

GIRAFFE

A giraffe does not have true horns, either. Its "horns," called ossicones, are not made of keratin. They are big bumps of bone on the giraffe's skull covered with skin and hair.

ANTLERS

Some hoofed animals *don't* have horns. Caribou, deer, elk, and moose grow antlers instead.

RED DEER

TULE ELK

Like horns, antlers grow in pairs on the top of the head. But unlike horns, they are not made of keratin. They are solid bone, covered with a furry protective skin called velvet. Antlers grow only in single pairs, and they can end in more than one point.

BLACK TAILED DEER

Antlers don't keep growing the way horns do. A new pair of antlers grows and falls off every year. New antlers are soft and spongy when they sprout in the spring. They harden as they grow longer over the summer.

By fall, antlers stop growing. By then, they are solid bone and no longer need a protective covering, so the velvet dries up and peels off.

ELK

KEY DEER

Caribou, deer, elk, and moose mate in the fall. The males fight one another with their newly hardened antlers to prove which is strongest. The winners get to mate; the losers have to wait until the next year to try again. Soon after the mating season ends, the antlers fall off. The next spring's new pair will grow in larger, with more branches and points.

Antlered animals are always male—with one exception: Both male and female caribou have antlers.

Moose grow the largest antlers of all. A full-grown moose can have a set as big as a bathtub!

MOOSE

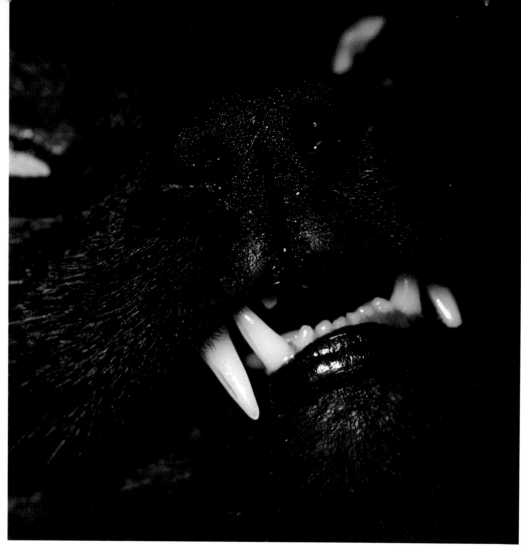

HOUSE CAT

FANGS

Fangs are special teeth. Although they grow in pairs inside the mouth, fangs are not used for eating. They are long, sharp, and pointed and are used for killing.

Many different kinds of animals have fangs, including bears, sea lions, cats, dogs and wolves, and even some kinds of bats and snakes. These animals are hunters and their fangs are deadly weapons. Both males and females have fangs.

When a bear shows its fangs like this, it means GO AWAY!

BROWN BEAR

CALIFORNIA SEA LIONS

When fighting among themselves, fanged animals sometimes settle arguments by baring their fangs at each other. The animal with the longer, sharper fangs usually wins, and the loser lives to fight another day.

A vampire bat uses its fangs to slice holes through its prey's fur and skin. Then it laps up the blood from the wounds with its long, rough tongue. Unlike the legendary monster, a vampire bat's bite is rarely fatal.

VAMPIRE BAT

TUSKS

Tusks are also a type of special teeth. They grow in pairs and extend far out of the mouth. These long, thick teeth can be used to dig food out of the ground, but they are not useful for chewing. Tusks are also called ivory.

PIG-DEER

WARTHOGS

Like horns and antlers, tusks are used in fights to push and jab. Both male and female animals may have tusks. But males' tusks grow bigger than females'. The males use them to fight and to protect their mates and young.

Elephants grow the biggest ivory. Their tusks can be ten feet long and weigh up to 200 pounds each. With huge tusks like these, elephants can easily topple trees and fend off hungry lions.

AFRICAN ELEPHANT

WALRUS

Walrus can use their tusks like giant ice picks to pull their heavy bodies out of the water and onto the slippery ice. They also glide on their tusks underwater while they suck up clams from the ocean floor.

DALL SHEEP

ROOSEVELT ELK

BROWN BEAR

AFRICAN ELEPHANT

All true horns, antlers, fangs, and tusks grow in pairs out of animals heads. They all end in points, and they all help animals find food and fight. But no two pairs of horns, antlers, fangs, or tusks are exactly alike. Each set is as unique as the individual animal they belong to.